# Tahiti & French Polynesia Travel Guide

Unveiling The French Polynesia: Best Attraction, Must See Sight, Things To Do, Where To Stay, Food, Culture And History Of Tahiti. Everything You Need To Know.

# Sarah H. Friedman

# Table Of Content

# Chapter 1. Introduction

## Welcome To Tahiti

As I went off the aeroplane onto the runway, a nice breeze stroked my hair and carried with it the beautiful perfume of sea and tropical blooms. The sun hung low in the sky, spreading a warm golden glow over whatever it touched. This was the moment I had been waiting for - my welcome to Tahiti, the paradise of the Pacific.

As I proceeded through the open-air airport, the vibrant sounds of ukuleles and Tahitian drums filled the air, forming a symphony that appeared to link with the very pulse of the island. The islanders greeted me with genuine smiles and the typical Polynesian rite of touching foreheads and noses, a display of connection and respect.

The turquoise waters of the lagoon lured in purity and beauty unlike anything I had ever seen before. I couldn't resist the temptation and soon found myself waist-deep in the surf, feeling the silky sand beneath my feet and the soothing caress of the waves. Schools of rainbow fish rushed around me, as if welcome me into their underwater home.

As the day faded to dusk, I made my way to the seaside, where a traditional Tahitian feast awaited. The aroma of roasted pig, fresh seafood, and exotic fruits filled the air. I joined the communal feast, sitting cross-legged on the mat, swapping anecdotes and laughter with both other guests and residents. It was a celebration of life, culture, and the simple joys of being in such a magnificent environment.

In the days that followed, I toured the island's gorgeous interior, hiking through deep woods to unearth hidden waterfalls and historic holy locations. Each step felt like a trip back in time, a connection to the spirit of Tahiti's ancestors who had previously travelled these precise routes.

And then there were the sunsets — the kind that artists seek to represent but can never fully duplicate. The sky morphed into a picture of burning oranges, deep purples, and delicate pinks, as if the gods themselves were putting on a show particularly for me.

My welcome to Tahiti wasn't only a physical arrival; it was an absorption into a world where time seemed to slow down, where nature and culture merged in a dance that was both old and ageless. As I stood on the shoreline, feeling the sand between my toes and the salt on my skin, I understood that this was more than merely a holiday – it was a soul-stirring moment that would eternally carry a piece of my heart.

## About the Book

### About This Guide: Tahiti Travel Guide 2023

Welcome to the perfect website for enjoying the magnificent island of Tahiti and the fascinating French Polynesia. Whether you're a first-time traveler or a seasoned adventurer, "Tahiti Travel Guide 2023: The Ultimate Guide to Exploring the Culture, Beaches, Cuisine, and Adventures of Tahiti and French Polynesia" is your compass to uncovering the treasures that await in this remote and stunning corner of the world.

Unveiling the Magic of Tahiti and Beyond:
Embark on a journey of discovery as this detailed book takes you through a meticulous exploration of not only Tahiti but also the lesser-known jewels of the French Polynesian archipelago. Dive deep into the rich culture, sun-kissed beaches, exquisite cuisine, and exciting activities that await you in this tropical haven.

Expert Insights and Practical Wisdom:
Authored by seasoned tourists and residents, this book is a combination of concepts that convey both information and personal anecdotes. You'll uncover useful advice on everything from when to travel for the finest experiences to how to spend sensibly, ensuring your holiday is both seamless and enjoyable.

Crafting Your Itinerary:
With in-depth suggestions for island hopping and designing your own tailor-made schedule, this book enables you

to personalise your trip depending on your interests and tastes. Whether you're seeking relaxation on magnificent beaches, immersion in local culture, or heart-pounding outdoor activities, this book is your guide.

Indulging in Tahitian Cuisine:
Delve into the world of Tahitian cuisine, where traditional dishes merge flavours of the sea and land. Navigate local markets and culinary culture to experience the intricate tapestry of tastes that constitute this region's gourmet environment.

Adventures of a Lifetime:
For thrill-seekers and environment connoisseurs, this book takes a thorough look at the diversity of activities available – from snorkeling and diving in crystal-clear oceans to hiking across pristine landscapes. Get ready to immerse yourself in the natural wonders and exhilarating adventures that Tahiti and French Polynesia offer.

Cultural Immersion and Island Treasures:
Venture beyond Tahiti to find the hidden gems of the French Polynesian archipelago. Gain insights into the local way of life, connect with the colorful past, and appreciate the worth of traditions that have been passed down through ages.

Practical Tips for Respectful Travel:
Navigate the local customs, etiquette, and communication intricacies with ease. This booklet offers critical information on language, safety, and cultural awareness to ensure your experiences with locals are respectful and meaningful.

Capturing Memories and Reflection:
Embrace the ambience of the islands by learning how to preserve your experience through photography and treasure your memories. This book also asks you to focus on the transformative effect of your Tahitian adventure.

Your Passport to Paradise:
"About This Guide: Tahiti Travel Guide 2023" is more than a compilation of information; it's your passport to a world of magnificent landscape, warm-hearted residents, and fantastic adventures. With this book in hand, you'll be ready to go on a vacation of a lifetime - one that promises to leave you with a deeper connection to the beauty and magic of Tahiti and French Polynesia.

## Discovering the Magic of Tahiti and French Polynesia

**Discovering the Magic of Tahiti and French Polynesia: A Journey Beyond Paradise**.

Tahiti and French Polynesia: a region that invokes visions of turquoise waters, palm-fringed shores, and the whispering of a tropical breeze. But beneath the postcard-perfect sights lies a fabric of magic that transcends the commonplace, enticing tourists to immerse themselves in a world where nature, culture, and the human spirit interweave.

A Symphony of Islands:
French Polynesia is an archipelago of 118 islands, each with its own distinct character and attraction. Tahiti, commonly termed "The Queen of the Pacific," is the core of this paradise, oozing a blend of urban dynamism and natural majesty. As you explore beyond Tahiti, you'll encounter hidden jewels like Bora Bora's overwater villas, Moorea's beautiful landscapes, and the pristine isolation of the Marquesas Islands.

The Spirit of Mana:
Tahiti's underlying charm resides in its relationship to the notion of "mana" — the life energy that runs through everything. From the swaying coconut palms to the

warm smiles of the residents, you'll feel this ethereal spirit embracing you at every step. It's in the repetitive beats of the drums, the hypnotic hula dance, and the ancient rituals that continue to define everyday life.

Cultural Resilience and Identity:
The culture of Tahiti and French Polynesia is a living monument to the endurance of its people. Rooted in Polynesian history, rituals, and stories, the islands give a look into a way of life that has persisted for millennia. Through language, tattoo artwork, and storytelling, residents proudly retain their identity while welcome tourists into their culture.

Beaches of Dreams:
Tahiti's beaches are more than merely stretches of sand and azure waters - they're doorways to tranquilly and adventure. Each beach has its personality: black sands meet colourful coral reefs on the eastern coast, while white sands caressed by moderate

waves form a perfect atmosphere for leisure on the western side.

Culinary Journeys:
Indulge your taste buds with the flavours of Tahitian cuisine, a combination of indigenous veggies, seafood, and unique spices. From the earthy umami of poisson cru (marinated raw fish) to the richness of tropical fruits, every taste offers a feeling of the islands' abundance. Engage with locals at food markets, where the fragrance of freshly produced dishes permeates the air, and culinary traditions are shared.

Beyond Boundaries:
Venturing beyond Tahiti leads you to the remote and unspoiled areas of French Polynesia. The Marquesas Islands, for instance, expose panoramas that seem to defy reality, with towering cliffs, green valleys, and ancient riches eager to be uncovered.

Preserving Paradise:
Exploring the magic of Tahiti and French Polynesia comes with a responsibility to conserve and maintain the delicate ecosystems and cultures that make this area remarkable. Sustainable tourism practices, recognising local customs, and supporting local communities all play a role in ensuring that the magic survives for decades to come.

"Discovering the Magic of Tahiti and French Polynesia" is more than a trip through a stunning setting; it's an excursion of the senses, emotions, and relationships. As you peruse the pages of this book, you'll find yourself enticed into a world where the natural and the cultural easily combine, leaving you with memories that will long recall the compelling magnetism of these islands.

# Chapter 2. Planning Your Trip

## When to Go: Best Times to Visit

### When to Go: Best Times to Visit Tahiti and French Polynesia

Choosing the right time to set foot on the paradisiacal shores of Tahiti and French Polynesia is crucial to ensure you experience the islands at their most enthralling. The weather, activity, and overall surroundings alter throughout the year, offering diverse flavours of this tropical haven. Here's a detailed guide to the optimal times to visit, mixed with a personal experience to show the charm of the islands.

1. Dry Season (April through October):
Personal Experience:
I embarked on my Tahitian tour in late May, just as the dry season was taking hold. As the plane plummeted, I was astonished by clear skies that highlighted the beautiful,

green plains beneath. This was the time when the islanders donned their most vibrant garments. The light breeze gave a lovely chill, making it great for visiting the beaches, hiking trails, and partaking in outdoor activities without the risk of unexpected downpours.

2. Whale-Watching Season (July to October):
Personal Experience:
During my visit in August, I had the great privilege of watching lovely humpback whales breaching and playing in the waters of Moorea. These gentle giants go to the warm waters of French Polynesia during this season, affording a rare opportunity for amazing encounters. It was an awe-inspiring encounter that left me humbled by the beauty of nature.

3. Shoulder Seasons (November and March):
Personal Experience:

My journey lasted until early November, just when the change from dry to wet season was commencing. While some uncommon rain showers graced the afternoons, they were typically short-lived, leaving the surroundings revitalised and bright. The fewer guests at this time meant that I could genuinely appreciate the calm of the beaches and take in the vistas without the hustle and bustle.

4. Wet Season (December to March):
Personal Experience:
As the year came to a climax, I found myself in Tahiti during the rainy season. While it's true that this time of year sees more rain, it also brings forth a lushness and green splendour that's unlike any other. The brief but heavy showers were often followed by breathtaking rainbows that spanned across the sky - a monument to the island's propensity to dazzle even in the thick of storm.

5. Consideration for Events:
Throughout the year, Tahiti hosts several events and festivals that give a broader insight into the local culture. The Heiva Festival in July celebrates traditional dance, music, and sports, while November's Hawaiki Nui Va'a Canoe Race gathers together paddlers from across the Pacific for a tough competition.

Selecting the optimum time to visit Tahiti and French Polynesia hinges on your interests and desired experiences. Whether you chose the dry season for its outdoor adventures, the whale-watching months for interactions with marine giants, or the shoulder seasons for a blend of solitude and lushness, each period brings its own distinct draw. With a well planned time to travel, you'll find yourself immersed in the enchantment of these islands, forming memories that will long be imprinted in your heart.

# Visa Requirements and Travel Essentials

## Visa Requirements and Travel Essentials for Tahiti and French Polynesia

Embarking on a cruise to the picturesque islands of Tahiti and French Polynesia is a dream come true, but it's crucial to be prepared with the right paperwork and travel needs to ensure a pleasant and hassle-free holiday. Here's an in-depth advice on visa requirements and the required products you should bring for your trip.

Visa Requirements:
Personal Experience:
When I scheduled my holiday to Tahiti, one of the first things I reviewed was the visa requirements. As a visitor, I heard that

various nationalities, including those from the US, Canada, and the EU, may enjoy visa-free stays of up to 90 days for tourism purposes. This made the planning process much easier, because I didn't have to worry about acquiring a visa in advance.

1. Passport Validity:
Ensure that your passport is valid for at least six months after your anticipated departure date from French Polynesia. Some airlines may not allow you to board the plane if your passport doesn't meet this criteria.

2. Return or Onward Ticket:
Immigration officers might demand proof of your plan to leave the country, such as a return or onward ticket. Make sure you have a copy of your flight itinerary handy.

3. Accommodation Details:
Although it's not normally needed, having evidence of your hotel arrangements for the

duration of your vacation could streamline the immigration process.

4. Visa Extensions:
If you intend to stay in French Polynesia for more than 90 days, you'll need to request for a visa extension at the local police station or gendarmerie before your initial 90 days are up.

Travel Essentials:
Personal Experience:
Packing for my Tahitian holiday involves a precise balance between practicality and the anticipation of enjoying the wonder of the islands. Here are some crucial things that made my journey comfortable and memorable.

1. Lightweight Clothing:
Pack lightweight, breathable garments suited for the tropical atmosphere. Don't forget to carry swimsuits, cover-ups, and comfortable walking shoes for sightseeing.

2. Sun Protection:
Sunscreen, sunglasses, and a wide-brimmed hat are needed to protect oneself from the intense tropical sun.

3. Insect Repellent:
The islands are blessed with beauty, however mosquitoes may sometimes be a problem. Pack a quality insect repellant to insure tranquil nights.

4. Adapters and Chargers:
French Polynesia utilises Type E and Type F power outlets, so make sure to pack the necessary adapters and chargers for your electrical equipment.

5. Medications and First Aid:
Carry any important prescription medicines, along with a basic first aid kit containing things like adhesive bandages, disinfecting wipes, and pain relievers.

6. Language Guidebook or App:
While English is frequently spoken in tourist locations, carrying a basic French language guidebook or app could boost your contact with locals.

7. Waterproof Gear:
Invest in waterproof backpacks or bags to secure your electronics and critical documents while aquatic activities.

8. Cash and Cards:
French Pacific Franc (XPF) is the local currency. While credit cards are accepted at many companies, it's a good idea to have some local currency on hand, especially when visiting smaller stores.

9. Snorkeling and Diving Gear:
If you're a fan of underwater exploration, consider bringing your own snorkeling mask and fins for a more comfortable and personalised experience.

Navigating visa processes and packing the necessary travel equipment are key stages in enjoying a memorable and joyful holiday to Tahiti and French Polynesia. By preparing in preparation and having everything you need on hand, you'll be ready to savour the beauty, culture, and magic that these islands have to offer.

## Budgeting for Your Tahiti Adventure

**Budgeting for Your Tahiti Adventure: A Comprehensive Guide**

Embarking on a cruise to the magnificent paradise of Tahiti and French Polynesia could be a dream come true, but it's necessary to plan your money properly to make the most of your adventure without any financial shocks. Here's an in-depth guide on budgeting for your Tahiti adventure, packed with guidance and insights to help you plan for a delightful and financially practical trip.

1. Flights:
Personal Experience:
When I purchased my tickets to Tahiti, I found that travel price ranged substantially dependent on the time of year and the airline. Planning early in advance and being flexible with trip dates allowed me to get a more affordable pricing.

2. Accommodation:
Personal Experience:
From upscale resorts to modest guesthouses, Tahiti has a range of hotel solutions to suit varied budgets. I picked for a blend of mid-range hotels and tiny guesthouses, which not only gave comfort but also, enabled me to experience the warmth of Tahitian hospitality.

3. Transportation:
Personal Experience:
Navigating Tahiti and its nearby islands could encompass several methods of

transportation, such as domestic flights, ferries, and local buses. Planning ahead and exploring numerous possibilities helped me identify cost-effective methods to travel about.

## 4. Meals & Dining:
Personal Experience:
Dining in Tahiti may vary from budget-friendly food trucks selling wonderful local foods to high-end restaurants with beautiful views. While I indulged myself to several fancy dinners, I also liked visiting local markets and trying out cheap street food choices.

## 5. Activities and Excursions:
Personal Experience:
One of the pleasures of my vacation was the number of activities and excursions offered in Tahiti - from snorkeling and diving to hiking and cultural tours. I put aside a budget for these events and prioritized the ones that connected best with my interests.

6. Souvenirs and Gifts:

Personal Experience:

Bringing back a bit of Tahiti as a souvenir was significant to me. I designated a part of my money for buying at local markets, where I bought unusual handicrafts, artwork, and traditional Tahitian pareos (sarongs).

7. Travel Insurance:

Personal Experience:

Travel insurance is an essential investment to protect yourself against unexpected events, such as trip cancellations, medical emergencies, or lost luggage. Researching numerous insurance alternatives and picking coverage that corresponds with your requirements is vital.

8. Currency Exchange and Cash Withdrawals:

Personal Experience:

French Pacific Franc (XPF) is the national currency of Tahiti. While credit cards are widely accepted, having some local money on hand for small purchases and gratuities is crucial. Research the most cost-effective options for currency exchange and ATM withdrawals.

9. Miscellaneous Expenses:
Budget for unplanned costs or incidental charges that may occur during your holiday. It's always preferable to include a cushion in your budget to allow for any unforeseen.
Budgeting for your Tahiti visit needs careful consideration of many components, from flights and hotel to activities and food. By preparing ahead, considering numerous alternatives, and picking activities that coincide with your interests, you can construct a budget that allows you to thoroughly immerse yourself in the beauty and magic of Tahiti and French Polynesia without compromising on financial peace of mind.

# Chapter 3. Getting to Tahiti

## Airports and Transportation Options

**Airports and Transportation Options in Tahiti and French Polynesia: Navigating Paradise**

Arriving in Tahiti signifies the beginning of a wonderful vacation through the lovely islands of French Polynesia. To make the most of your trip, identifying the airports and transportation alternatives available is crucial. Here's a complete guide, coupled with a personal experience, to aid you travel this magnificent refuge.

Airports:
Personal Experience:
Stepping off the aeroplane at Faa'a International Airport in Tahiti was a bizarre

feeling. The warm tropical breeze swiftly engulfed me, and the sight of the stunning scenery in the distance set the tone for the adventure ahead. The airport's open-air design harmoniously merged with the island's natural magnificence, offering an experience of arrival unlike any other.

1. Faa'a International Airport (PPT):
This is the major international entry to Tahiti and French Polynesia. It's located just a short drive from the capital city, Papeete. The airport features modern facilities, including shops, restaurants, and currency exchange services.

Domestic Airports:
Personal Experience:
From Tahiti, I got on a short domestic flight to tour other islands in the archipelago. Moorea, Bora Bora, and Huahine are just a few examples of the areas that are conveniently accessible by domestic flights.

Transportation Options:
Personal Experience:
Navigating transportation possibilities in Tahiti was an adventure in itself. While leasing a car is a popular choice for solo exploration, I elected to employ a combination of local transportation and organised trips to go around.

1. Rental Cars:
Renting a car provides the ability to explore at your own pace. The main island of Tahiti has well-maintained highways, making it relatively straightforward to drive. Keep in mind that driving is on the right side of the road.

2. Taxis and Shuttles:
Taxis are available at the airports and in major cities. Shared shuttles provide quick transfers to and from accommodations. Negotiating fares in advance is suggested.

3. Public Buses:

Public buses are a cost-effective technique to travel between settlements on the larger islands. The bus system on Tahiti is trustworthy, and while the timing might be erratic, it's a good chance to communicate with people.

4. Ferries and Boats:
For island hopping, ferries and boats are necessary. High-speed boats and catamarans connect Tahiti with surrounding islands, giving stunning views of the coastline throughout the voyage.

5. Guided Tours & Excursions:
Personal Experience:
One of the delights of my holiday was having guided tours that allowed me to explore Tahiti's natural beauty and cultural tradition. Whether it was a snorkeling trip, a guided walk, or a traditional Polynesian dance show, each event was enriched by the expertise of the local guides.

Navigating airports and transportation alternatives in Tahiti and French Polynesia is a significant feature of your vacation through this tropical paradise. Embrace the spirit of adventure as you pick the transportation type that best suits your interests, and enable each excursion, whether by air, land, or sea, become a part of the memories you'll carry back from this amazing country.

## Navigating Local Transport

### Navigating Local Transport in Tahiti and French Polynesia: Embracing Island Life

Exploring the gorgeous landscapes and colourful cultures of Tahiti and French Polynesia necessitates a comprehensive dive into the local travel possibilities. From traditional buses to creative means of island hopping, here's a full guide to managing local transportation and immersing yourself in the rhythm of island life.

1. Le Truck:
Personal Experience:
Experiencing Tahitian local transportation wouldn't have been complete without a journey on a colourful "Le Truck." These open-sided buses, adorned with vibrant artwork, give an authentic and budget-friendly way to travel the islands.

2. Public Buses:
Personal Experience:
Public buses, known as "Le Truck" in Tahiti, are an important mode of mobility for both inhabitants and visitors. While the schedules might be informal, these buses connect significant towns and landmarks, allowing you to witness Tahitian life up close.

3. Renting Bicycles:
Personal Experience:

Renting a bicycle on the bigger islands, such as Tahiti or Moorea, may be a pleasant way to explore at your own pace. With generally flat terrain, you may cycle through villages, along coastlines, and even visit stunning vistas.

4. Taxis and Shuttles:
Personal Experience:
Taxis and shuttle services are readily available, particularly near airports and significant tourist attractions. Negotiating the charge in advance is usual, and taxis give a pleasant and handy means to move about.

5. Domestic Flights:
Personal Experience:
For island hopping or visiting more secluded places, domestic planes are necessary. While they bring convenience, they also afford great aerial vistas of the lovely landscape below.

6. Inter-Island Ferries:

Personal Experience:
Island hopping in French Polynesia wouldn't be complete without a boat adventure. High-speed ferries connect major islands, delivering both a practical method of travel and a gorgeous journey over blue waters.

7. Water Taxis:
Personal Experience:
Water taxis provide a unique way to travel between smaller islands or to explore locations not accessible by ordinary boats. These smaller boats provide a personal experience and an opportunity to explore the magnificent coastlines.

8. Guided Tours:
Personal Experience:
Opting for guided trips not only provides hassle-free transportation but also brings insights and remarks from local guides. Whether it's a snorkeling expedition or a

cultural tour, guided activities create a deeper connection to the environment.

9. Embracing Local Connections:
Personal Experience:
During my travels, I learned that utilising local transport not only permitted me to see Tahiti's beauty but also offered me the chance to interact with lovely islanders. From striking up talks on buses to swapping experiences with fellow passengers, these encounters enhanced my journey.

Navigating local transportation in Tahiti and French Polynesia is an essential component of embracing the island way of life. Whether you're getting on a "Le Truck," riding along coastal trails, or floating on a boat, each form of travel delivers a fresh perspective on the natural beauty, culture, and community that characterize these magnificent islands.

# Chapter 4. Exploring Tahiti

## Unveiling Tahiti's Rich Cultural Heritage

**Unveiling Tahiti's Rich Cultural Heritage: A Journey into Tradition and Authenticity**

Tahiti's attraction extends far beyond its gorgeous scenery; it's a site that lures tourists to look into its rich cultural past. From ancient traditions to present expressions, Tahiti delivers a tapestry of experiences that communicate the heart and soul of the island. Here's a thorough tour of Tahiti's cultural past, enabling you to discover the legends, artworks, and practises that make this wonderful land.

1. Traditional Dance and Music:
Personal Experience:
Witnessing a traditional Tahitian dance performance was a thrilling highlight of my

vacation. The swinging hips, rhythmic drumming, and vibrant costumes revealed stories of mythology, ceremonies, and feasts that had been passed down through years.

2. Heiva Festival:
Personal Experience:
Attending the annual Heiva Festival was a thorough immersion into Tahitian culture. Held in July, this month-long celebration features traditional dance, music, sports, and crafts. I astonished by the talent of dancers, the intricate beauty of tattoo designs, and the sense of brotherhood that dominated the festivities.

3. Marae: Ancient Temples:
Personal Experience:
Exploring the marae, historic sacred spots, helped me to go back in time and connect with the spiritual beliefs of Tahiti's forebears. These stone structures, traditionally places of prayer and ritual, are

a tribute to the ongoing cultural relevance of the island.

4. Tapa Cloth and Artistry:
Personal Experience:
Learning about the process of creating tapa cloth, a traditional sort of fabric produced from the bark of trees, was a voyage into handicraft. Witnessing artisans at work, applying ancient ways to generate magnificent patterns, deepened my knowledge for Tahiti's cultural history.

5. Language and Storytelling:
Personal Experience:
Engaging with individuals in Tahitian, the local language, established a unique connection to the culture. I listened to stories passed down through generations, finding the myths that are linked with the sites I was investigating.

6. Tattoo Tradition:
Personal Experience:

Tahiti's tattoo culture is a living art form that communicates personal experiences and cultural tales. I had the privilege of learning about the complicated designs, their importance, and the skill required to produce tattoos that are both physically beautiful and emotionally important.

7. Local Markets and Cuisine:
Personal Experience:
Exploring local markets, I was introduced to the blend of flavours that characterise Tahitian cuisine. From eating exotic fruits to relishing in delicacies like poisson cru (marinated raw fish), each swallow was a celebration of Tahiti's culinary heritage.

8. Living Traditions:
Personal Experience:
Tahiti's cultural past is not consigned to museums; it's a vibrant, breathing part of everyday life. From the warmth of people greeting you with a traditional nose kiss (hongi) to seeing dance performances

during community festivals, the island's traditions are woven into the fabric of daily life.

9. Cultural Exchange and Respect:
Personal Experience:
Engaging nicely with locals encouraged me to obtain deeper insights into their way of life. Learning basic Tahitian language and learning local norms enhanced bonds and insured that my interactions were meaningful and authentic.

Unveiling Tahiti's rich cultural past is a trip of discovery, respect, and connection. As you explore traditional dance, marae, artwork, and legends, you'll find that Tahiti's soul goes beyond its outer beauty. It's a setting where traditions are cherished, where the past and present dance together, enticing you to be a part of its tapestry of culture and authenticity.

# Must-Visit Beaches and Their Unique Charms

## Must-Visit Beaches and Their Unique Charms in Tahiti: A Paradise of Shores

Tahiti's beaches are more than merely gorgeous stretches of sand and azure oceans; each one possesses its own personality, history, and charm. Embarking on a visit to these coastal jewels is an invitation to uncover a rich tapestry of beauty. Here's a complete guide to six must-visit beaches in Tahiti, packed with a personal experience that captures the essence of their distinct attractions.

1. Matira Beach, Bora Bora:

Personal Experience:

Setting foot on Matira Beach was like stumbling upon a vision come to life. The powdery white sand met the crystal-clear waters in a beautiful blend of hues. As I went along the shore, I couldn't resist the allure of the water, and I found myself immersed in a warm embrace that was both relaxing and exhilarating.

2. Temae Beach, Moorea:
Personal Experience:
Temae Beach's attractiveness resides on its calm beauty. Backed by lush forest and with stunning views of Moorea's peaks, it's a refuge of calm. I spent hours reclining under the shade of palm trees, savouring the sweet caress of the air and watching the ever-changing colours of the lagoon.

3. La Plage de Maui, Tahiti:
Personal Experience:
La Plage de Maui, with its famed black sands, preserves a peculiar mystery.

Surrounded by towering volcanic terrain, this beach emits an air of wildness. Watching the waves crash against the dark beach, I was reminded of the vast forces of nature that have formed these islands.

4. Tiahura Beach, Moorea:
Personal Experience:
Tiahura Beach, with its peaceful waves and magnificent coral gardens, is an underwater paradise for snorkeling fanatics. I began on a wonderful snorkeling excursion, watching a kaleidoscope of marine life beneath the surface – a symphony of colors and life that left me in astonishment.

5. Taharuu Beach, Tahiti:
Personal Experience:
Taharuu Beach is a haven for surfers and anyone seeking a connection with the ocean's energy. As I watched surfers ride the waves, I felt a deep appreciation for the way Tahiti's natural components deliver both exhilaration and a sense of harmony with the environment.

6. Rangiroa Beaches, Tuamotu Atolls:
Personal Experience:
On the remote atoll of Rangiroa, I saw beaches that looked unspoiled by time. The shores looked to continue into eternity, and the experience of remoteness was both humbling and powerful. Here, the beaches muttered stories of seclusion and the rhythm of living governed by the tides.

7. Lagoonarium Beach, Moorea:
Personal Experience:

Lagoonarium Beach is a refuge of tranquilly, providing the ability to swim with an array of marine species in a natural lagoon setting. Snorkeling here was like entering a hidden planet, where fish of all sizes and colors whirled around me, creating a symphony of underwater joy.

8. Fare Beach, Huahine:
Personal Experience:
Fare Beach on Huahine intrigued me with its rustic attractiveness. As I went along the shore, I encountered the warmth of local hospitality, with tiny food carts providing freshly prepared treats. It was a peep into the simplicity and honesty of Tahitian life.

Exploring Tahiti's must-visit beaches is a study of variation – from the perfect sands to the wild shores. Each beach holds its own narrative, presenting a specific facet of Tahiti's natural beauty. As you sink your toes into the sands, bask in the sun's warmth, or dive beneath the surface, you'll find that the beaches of Tahiti are not merely destinations; they are portals to extraordinary experiences and the heart of this paradise.

## Crafting Your Ideal Itinerary for Island Hopping

**Crafting Your Ideal Itinerary for Island Hopping in Tahiti: A Journey Through Paradise**

Island hopping in Tahiti and French Polynesia is a dream come true, allowing you to encounter a patchwork of landscapes, cultures, and experiences. Crafting the perfect agenda needs a careful balance between relaxation and activity, discovery and immersion. Here's an entire guide to help you construct your ideal island-hopping plan, along with a thorough example that embodies the essence of this fantastic adventure.

1. Research and Prioritize:

Begin by researching the islands of French Polynesia to discover their individual traits. Decide what experiences mean most to you - whether it's stunning beaches, undersea adventure, cultural immersion, or a blend of everything.

2. Choose Your Islands:

Example Itinerary:

• Days 1-3: Tahiti: Start your holiday in Tahiti, seeing Papeete's markets and cultural attractions. Venture into the picturesque interior, walk to waterfalls, and enjoy Tahitian cuisine.

• Days 4-6: Moorea: Hop over to Moorea, where you may bathe in the lagoon, walk to viewpoints, and experience local traditions.

• Days 7-9: Bora Bora: Fly to Bora Bora for overwater villas, water activities, and a romantic sunset cruise.

• Days 10-12: Huahine: Discover the authenticity of Huahine, where you may bike around the island, meet people, and relax on secluded beaches.

3. Travel Logistics:
Consider aeroplane timings, boat connections, and travel time between islands. Book flights and hotels well in advance, especially during peak seasons.

4. Embrace Variety:
Include a mix of relaxation and adventure. Balance beach days with cultural visits, snorkeling with hiking, and leisurely exploration with heart-pounding activities.

5. Allow for Flexibility:
Leave room for spontaneity. If you fall in love with an island, allow yourself the freedom to stay longer. If you uncover a secret gem not on your itinerary, be open to adjusting your plans.

6. Plan Rest Days:

Island hopping may be fun, but it's vital to avoid burnout. Include leisure days where you may sunbathe on the beach, read a book, or simply enjoy the calm of your surroundings.

7. Connect with Locals:
Engage with locals to discover their way of life and acquire insights into the culture. Participate in local activities, visit markets, and attend cultural events.

8. Capture Moments:
Don't forget to schedule time for photography and relaxation. Sunrises, sunsets, and stargazing in this remote paradise are moments you'll want to remember.

9. Respect the Environment:
Tahiti's unspoilt beauty is vulnerable. Engage in appropriate tourism behaviours, such as reef-safe sunscreen and conserving marine life during water activities.

10. Reflect on Your Journey:

Example Itinerary:

• Day 13: Return to Tahiti for your departure. Spend your last day reflecting on your experience, potentially with a beachfront picnic or a visit to a local artisan shop to acquire souvenirs.

Crafting the ideal island-hopping schedule in Tahiti and French Polynesia is an art that needs careful consideration of your interests, preferences, and the particular attractions of each site. Whether you're inclined to adventure, cultural activities, or tranquil beaches, picking a well-balanced plan assures that every day is a new chapter in your vacation across this beautiful island.

# Chapter 5. Savoring Cuisine

## Indulging in Traditional Tahitian Dishes

**Indulging in Traditional Tahitian Dishes: A Culinary Voyage Through Culture**

Exploring Tahiti and French Polynesia is not only a visual feast but a gourmet adventure that tantalizes the taste senses with different flavours and scents. Traditional Tahitian cuisine are a reflection of the islands' rich history, indigenous resources, and cultural legacy. Embark on a gastronomic trip as we dive deeper into the domain of traditional Tahitian food, coupled with a personal experience that captures the essence of delighting in these delightful pleasures.

1. Poisson Cru (Raw Fish Salad):
Personal Experience:

Sitting at a beach café in Moorea, I had my first interaction with poisson cru. The tray before me featured a fantastic arrangement of chopped raw fish, marinated in lime juice and coconut milk, adorned with bright greens. The early distrust gave way to pure joy as I absorbed the symphony of textures and the surge of freshness - a real reflection of Tahiti's natural richness.

2. Firi Firi (Tahitian Doughnuts):
Personal Experience:
Walking through a small market in Papeete, I came upon a shop selling firi firi - miniature, fried doughnuts topped with powdered sugar. The vendor's warm grin and the tempting aroma tempted me in. As I had my first taste, the crispy surface gave way to a soft, fluffy middle, and I knew why firi firi is a treasured delicacy among locals.

3. Poulet Fafa (Chicken Cooked in Taro Leaves):
Personal Experience:

In a tiny village café on Huahine, I ordered poulet fafa, a dish that emphasises the blend of Tahitian and Polynesian flavours. The tender chicken, wrapped in taro leaves and slow-cooked, absorbed the earthy richness of the leaves, providing a symphony of taste that accentuated Tahiti's agricultural past.

4. Uru (Breadfruit):
Personal Experience:
Uru, a starchy fruit, is a cornerstone in Tahitian cuisine. At a traditional feast, I had the opportunity to try numerous uru specialties, from grilled slices to mashed sides. The versatility of uru in both sweet and savory dishes showed its relevance in Tahitian culture and cuisine.

5. E'ia Ota (Coconut Seafood Salad):
Personal Experience:
Indulging in e'ia ota, a salad of shellfish marinated in coconut milk, put me on a sensory adventure. The smoothness of the coconut, along with the ocean-fresh fish,

offered a delicate blend of flavours that complemented the coastal grandeur of the islands.

6. Faraoa Po'e (Tahitian Fruit Pudding):
Personal Experience:
At a Tahitian feast, faraoa po'e took the attention as the dessert dish. The dessert, prepared from local fruits like bananas and papayas, was sweetened with vanilla and coated in banana leaves. With each taste, I admired the delicacy of the islands and the warmth of ancient methods.

7. Connection between the Land and Sea:
Personal Experience:
The essence of indulging in traditional Tahitian dishes goes beyond flavour - it's a connection to the land and sea that supports the culture. Engaging with local cooks and sharing tales about the ingredients boosted my appreciation for the authenticity of the meal.

Indulging in traditional Tahitian delights is a way to uncovering the heart and soul of the islands. From the raw fish salad to the exquisite desserts, each bite is a testimony to the rich cultural past and the close bond between the people, their environment, and their culinary traditions. As you enjoy the flavors of Tahiti, you'll journey on a tour that nourishes both body and soul, leaving you with memories that remain long beyond the final mouthful.

## Exploring Local Markets and Food Culture

**Exploring Local Markets and Food Culture in Tahiti: A Feast for the Senses**

Immersing yourself in the vivid tapestry of Tahitian culture extends beyond stunning landscapes; it penetrates to the centre of the islands' gourmet culture. Local markets are centres of activity, where the essence of Tahiti comes alive through colorful displays of fresh food, scented spices, and the dynamic dialogues between inhabitants and visitors. Join me as I dive deeper into the fascinating world of visiting local markets and culinary culture in Tahiti, combined with a personal experience that brings this sensory excursion to life.

1. Papeete Market:
Personal Experience:
Stepping into Papeete Market was like entering a kingdom of magic. The air was filled with a symphony of scents – rich tropical fruits, aromatic spices, and freshly baked bread. I strolled passed rows of kiosks covered with vivid flowers, sophisticated handicrafts, and, of course, a profusion of gourmet delicacies. The friendly chatting of merchants, the laughter of buyers, and the vibrant colors generated an ambiance that gripped me like an old friend.

2. Discovering Exotic Fruits:
Personal Experience:
At a market stall, I saw exotic fruits I had never seen before - rambutan, breadfruit, and soursop. Curiosity prompted me to sample each one, and with each swallow, I felt like I was devouring a portion of Tahiti's natural diversity. The fruits were a pleasant reminder that the islands are a treasure mine of flavours waiting to be found.

3. Engaging with Local Artisans:
Personal Experience:
Interacting with local crafters was a highlight of my market trip. I witnessed professional craftspeople weave gorgeous baskets and carve wooden sculptures, retaining traditional techniques that have been passed down through ages. Their narratives and creativity offered a higher degree of appreciation to the souvenirs I obtained.

4. Sampling Street Food:
Personal Experience:
The scent of sizzling food trucks drew me to examine Tahiti's street food culture. I dined on wonderful crepes packed with ham, cheese, and fresh vegetables, and my taste senses danced with joy. The food trucks were not only a gourmet treat but also a glimpse into the local eating culture that thrives in these open-air markets.

5. Traditional Dishes and Local Flavors:
Personal Experience:
At a market booth, I had the opportunity of eating classic Tahitian cuisine like poisson cru and breadfruit salad. The flavours were an embodiment of the islands' culinary tradition - the acidity of lime, the richness of coconut, and the earthiness of locally grown products.

6. Connecting with Locals:
Personal Experience:

The soul of exploring local markets rests in the interactions with the people who make Tahiti home. Conversations with merchants revealed not merely the provenance of their wares but also snippets of life on the islands. Their warmth and eagerness to share their stories brought depth to my understanding of Tahitian culture.

Exploring local markets and culinary culture in Tahiti is a multimodal excursion that stimulates your taste buds, engages your curiosity, and ties you to the heart of the islands. From the bustling bustle of the market booths to the flavors that tell stories of history and inventiveness, this gastronomic adventure is a feast for the senses and a window to the actual essence of Tahitian culture.

# Chapter 6. Adventures Await

## Water Sports & Activities: Snorkeling, Diving, Surfing

### Water Sports and Activities in Tahiti: Embracing the Ocean's Playground

Tahiti's magnificent oceans are not merely for admiring from the shore; they urge explorers to venture into a world of aquatic wonders. From the beautiful coral gardens to the exhilarating surf, water sports and activities in Tahiti give a range of experiences that connect you directly with the ocean. Join me as I explore extensively into the topic of snorkeling, diving, and surfing, coupled with a personal experience that reflects the essence of these aquatic events.

1. Snorkeling at Lagoon Paradises:
Personal Experience:

Floating above the coral gardens of Moorea's lagoon, I felt like I was suspended in a living artwork. The clarity of the water exhibited a tapestry of hues - schools of fish darting through the corals, exquisite rays floating by, and the unusual sight of an inquisitive sea turtle. Snorkeling in Tahiti's lagoons was an immersion into a world that looked both calm and full of life.

2. Diving into Underwater Realms:
Personal Experience:
Descending into the depths of Bora Bora's lagoon, I ventured into a realm where time seemed to stand still. The beauty of the coral formations, the dance of sunlight spilling through the water, and the sense of weightlessness provided an extraordinary experience. Exploring shipwrecks and discovering unusual aquatic animals was like unravelling the ocean's secrets.

3. Riding the Waves: Surfing:
Personal Experience:

Paddling out to catch the waves of Teahupo'o, I realised I was going to experience the raw ferocity of Tahiti's surf. As the wave arrived, I rode it with a mix of joy and awe. The rush of adrenaline, the impression of floating above the water's surface, and the backdrop of gorgeous surroundings produced a connection to nature that was both exciting and humbling.

4. Guided Snorkeling and Diving Tours:
Personal Experience:
Joining guided outings boosted my water activities to new heights. Expert guides brought me to hidden snorkeling sites and diving places brimming with life. Their awareness of the marine ecology and their drive for conservation offered a layer of information to the experience, improving my appreciation for Tahiti's underwater beauty.

5. Cultural Water Activities:
Personal Experience:

Participating in traditional water activities like outrigger canoeing gives insights into Tahiti's past. As I paddled alongside natives, I discovered about the traditional methods used for navigation and the deep relationship between the Tahitian people and the ocean.

6. Connecting with Nature:
Personal Experience:
The lure of water sports and activities in Tahiti is not merely the enjoyment; it's the potential to connect with nature on a basic level. Each interaction with marine life, each wave conquered, and each second spent beneath the surface reminded me of the delicate balance that exists between human and ocean.

Water sports and activities in Tahiti are a celebration of the ocean's majesty and its secrets waiting to be discovered. Snorkeling, diving, and surfing are not only physical hobbies; they are portals to understanding the organisms that exist beneath the waves. As you enjoy these aquatic expeditions, you'll come face to face with the awe-inspiring magnificence of Tahiti's underwater areas, making memories that will long be imprinted in your heart.

## Hiking Through Lush Landscapes and Hidden Gems

**Hiking Through Lush Landscapes and Hidden Gems in Tahiti: Nature's Grand Tapestry**

Tahiti's attraction extends beyond its beaches; its lush landscapes and hidden roads entice guests to experience a world of natural beauty and isolation. Hiking through the lush hills, you'll find hidden treasures, spectacular landscapes, and the vibrant heart of the islands. Join me for a comprehensive analysis of hiking in Tahiti, combined with a personal experience that captures the character of these fascinating paths.

1. Fautaua Valley Trail:
Personal Experience:
Embarking on the Fautaua Valley Trail was like entering a place unspoiled by time. The road brought me through beautiful foliage, across bubbling streams, and into the arms of towering trees. As I ascended farther into the valley, the sound of the cascade increased louder, and the sight of Fautaua Falls tumbling down the rocks left me in wonder. The excursion was not only a physical one; it was a spiritual connection to nature's majesty.

2. Three Coconut Trees Pass:
Personal Experience:
Traversing the Three Coconut Trees Pass, I was welcomed with amazing views that stretched across lush valleys, azure streams, and distant peaks. As I stood beneath the shade of those legendary coconut trees, I felt

a profound sensation of loneliness and oneness with the natural world.

3. Cross-Island Trail:
Personal Experience:
Hiking the Cross-Island Trail was a tour of contrasts. Starting in lush woodland regions, I soon emerged into open meadows with spectacular panoramas. The descent brought me to hidden grottos and freshwater springs, where I could chill myself and ponder on the richness of Tahiti's terrain.

4. Belvedere Lookout, Moorea:
Personal Experience:
Reaching the Belvedere Lookout on Moorea was a moment of triumph. The drive through tropical bush rewarded me with a stunning view of Opunohu and Cook's Bays, bordered by towering hills. It was a reminder of the amazing magnificence that Tahiti's interior possesses.

5. Pari Coast Trail:
Personal Experience:
The Pari Coast Trail gives a view into the wild side of Tahiti. As I proceeded along the rugged beach, the waves pounding against the rocks and the salty breeze electrified my senses. The stroll led to calm coves and tidal pools that felt like hidden havens.

6. Connecting with Nature:
Personal Experience:
Hiking in Tahiti enabled me to disengage from the world and reconnect with nature in its purest form. The rustling leaves, the symphony of birdcalls, and the sensation of soil beneath my feet formed a sensory experience that was both grounding and exhilarating.

Hiking through lush landscapes and hidden treasures in Tahiti is an excursion that puts you into the heart of nature's magnificent tapestry. Each trail is a chapter waiting to be written - a tale of adventure, discovery, and a profound connection to the planet. As you journey through mountains, valleys, and beachfront roads, you'll encounter the hidden jewels that make Tahiti not just a holiday, but a haven for individuals seeking the embrace of the natural world.

## Connecting with Nature: Wildlife and Ecotourism

### Connecting with Nature in Tahiti: Embracing Wildlife and Ecotourism

Tahiti's attraction extends beyond its magnificent beauty; it's a spot where the interaction between people and the natural world is firmly appreciated. Embracing animals and participation in ecotourism activities help you to create a profound contact with the environment, producing a sense of concern for the fragile ecosystems that differentiate these islands. Join me as I delve further into the area of connecting with nature through animal encounters and ecotourism experiences, combined with a personal trip that captures the essence of this profound connection.

1. Swimming with Marine Life:
Personal Experience:
Snorkeling in Tahiti's lagoons, I found myself swimming alongside a gentle giant – a gorgeous manta ray. Its wings glided over the sea with an elegance that left me in awe. The conference was a reminder of the delicate dance between humans and aquatic animals, imploring us to maintain and protect the underwater environment.

2. Whale Watching:
Personal Experience:
On a whale-watching tour, I was thrilled by the sight of humpback whales breaching and playing in the open ocean. The energy and force of these gorgeous creatures were a sobering reminder of the interdependence

of all life beings, and the need of conserving their ecosystems.

3. Birdwatching and Avian Sanctuaries:
Personal Experience:
Exploring Tahiti's gorgeous landscapes, I encountered avian sanctuaries that offered shelter for endangered bird species. The sound of beautiful birdcalls and the sight of colorful plumage provided a symphony of beauty to my travels, highlighting the significance of maintaining biodiversity.

4. Participating in Coral Conservation:
Personal Experience:
Joining a coral conservation programme, I gained the opportunity to contribute to the health of Tahiti's coral reefs. Under the direction of marine biologists, I studied about coral restoration techniques and observed firsthand the influence of human activities on these fragile ecosystems.

5. Sustainable Eco-Tours:

Personal Experience:
Participating in sustainable eco-tours allowed me to view the beauty of Tahiti while minimising my affect on the environment. Whether kayaking through mangrove forests or climbing with experienced guides, these experiences generated a sense of responsibility for the environment I was experiencing.

6. Immersion in Local Communities:
Personal Experience:
Engaging with local communities and indigenous peoples expanded my knowledge of the symbiotic relationship they have with the planet. Through their stories, traditions, and rituals, I gathered insights into the harmonious coexistence that has distinguished Tahiti's culture for millennia.

7. Reflecting on the Journey:
Personal Experience:
Connecting with nature in Tahiti was not just about the interactions; it was about the

insights they provided. As I stood on a lovely beach, surrounded by pure beauty, I recognised that my experiences were not only treasured recollections but also a call to action - a call to conserve the very ecosystems that had touched my heart.

Connecting with nature through animal encounters and ecotourism in Tahiti is an invitation to be a responsible guardian of the world. It's a chance to move beyond the position of a spectator and become an active participant in the safeguarding of Earth's treasures. As you swim with marine life, see whales dance, and immerse yourself in lush ecosystems, you'll not only generate amazing experiences but also develop a deeper appreciation for the delicate balance that preserves life on these wonderful islands.

# Chapter 7. Experiencing French Polynesia

## Exploring Beyond Tahiti: Island Gems and Atolls

### Exploring Beyond Tahiti: Island Gems and Atolls Unveiled

While Tahiti is a paradise in its own right, the appeal of French Polynesia reaches far beyond its principal island. Venturing to the lesser-known island gems and faraway atolls finds a world of pristine beauty, rich culture, and secret treasures waiting to be discovered. Join me as I dive deeper into the experience of visiting beyond Tahiti, complimented with a personal adventure that captures the allure of these island gems and atolls.

## 1. Bora Bora: The Jewel of the Pacific:

Personal Experience:

Arriving to Bora Bora felt like entering into a dream. The beautiful turquoise lagoon, crowned by the towering peak of Mount Otemanu, was a spectacle that seemed unattainable. Snorkeling among the coral gardens and sunbathing in an overwater home, I was engulfed in a sensation of luxury and natural beauty that Bora Bora is famous for.

## 2. Rangiroa: Diving into the Depths:

Personal Experience:

Descending into Rangiroa's lagoon, I was met with a world of aquatic magnificence. The atoll's coral walls dropped precipitously into the abyss, exposing a stunning array of aquatic life. The currents drove me into underwater canyons, where I saw sharks, dolphins, and schools of colorful fish - a witness to Rangiroa's reputation as a diving paradise.

## 3. Tikehau: A Secluded Paradise:

**Personal Experience:**

Tikehau delighted me with its untouched beauty and tranquil ambiance. The pink sand beaches and crystal-clear oceans were a panacea for the soul. As I snorkeled in the lagoon, I found myself surrounded by an underwater Eden, where beautiful corals and an abundance of fish created a mesmerising tapestry.

## 4. Huahine: The Garden of Eden:

**Personal Experience:**

Huahine appeared like a secret paradise aching to be uncovered. Biking throughout the island's stunning scenery, I spotted marae (ancient temples), vanilla plantations, and traditional settlements. The compassion of the citizens and the reality of ordinary life formed a picture of a paradise that embraced both history and technology.

## 5. Fakarava: Seclusion and Serenity:

**Personal Experience:**

Fakarava's remote appeal put a spell on me when I arrived on its beaches. The unspoilt beaches and gorgeous oceans were matched only by the tranquilly that engulfed the atoll. As I stared at the great expanse of the night sky, unmarred by city lights, I understood that Fakarava was a paradise for persons seeking seclusion and connection with nature.

6. Aitutaki: A Polynesian Gem:
Personal Experience:
Crossing into Aitutaki's lagoon, I was enchanted by its ethereal beauty. The motus (islets) surrounded by azure oceans were like a vision come to life. Sailing to One Foot Island, I marveled at the pure beauty and the sensation of timelessness that Aitutaki radiates.

7. Immersion in Local Cultures:
Personal Experience:
Exploring beyond Tahiti was not simply about sight; it was about engaging with local

cultures. From participating in traditional dance performances to mastering the craft of weaving, I understood that each island has its own special traditions and narratives to give.

Exploring beyond Tahiti is a voyage that exhibits the different and magnificent treasures of French Polynesia. Each island gem and atoll is a world unto itself, demanding to be explored, worshipped, and stitched into the fabric of your memories. As you travel beyond the beaches of Tahiti, you'll discover that French Polynesia is a constellation of paradise, each island a sparkling star in a celestial tapestry of beauty and magic.

## Cultural Immersion in the Archipelago

### Cultural Immersion in the Archipelago: Unveiling the Heart of French Polynesia

Beyond the breathtaking landscape and pure waters, French Polynesia includes a cultural richness that urges travellers to mingle, connect, and become a part of its dynamic tapestry. Cultural immersion in the archipelago is an invitation to explore into the traditions, art, music, and way of life that have been cultivated for generations. Join me on a full exploration of cultural immersion in French Polynesia, combined with a personal experience that embodies the essence of this unique partnership.

1. Traditional Dance and Music:
Personal Experience:
As I observed a traditional Tahitian dance performance, I felt the rhythm of the drums vibrate inside me. The dancers' delicate motions told stories of the islands' history, mythology, and customs. The music seems to communicate the entire soul of the civilisation, and I couldn't help but sway to its captivating melodies.

2. Marae: Ancient Temples and Sacred Sites:
Personal Experience:
stepping among the old marae – stone platforms used for spiritual and communal gatherings – was like stepping into the footsteps of history. The aura of devotion that enveloped these areas offered a glimpse into the spiritual link that the Tahitian people had with their ancestors and the environment.

3. Art and Craftsmanship:
Personal Experience:
Visiting a local artisan's workshop, I saw as gorgeous designs were woven into baskets and tapa cloths. The craftsmanship displayed the deep-rooted ingenuity that defined Tahitian art. Engaging with artists, I understood that each piece holds a bit of the islands' legends and traditions.

4. Traditional Navigation and Outrigger Canoeing:
Personal Experience:

Navigating the lagoon in an outrigger canoe was a tutorial in traditional navigation techniques. The skillful supervision of the indigenous permitted me to undertake a journey that the progenitors of French Polynesia previously embarked through. As I paddled, I understood the deep tie between the people and the river that sustains them.

5. Heiva: A Celebration of Culture:
Personal Experience:
Participating in the annual Heiva event was an immersion into the centre of Tahitian culture. The bright parades, traditional sports, and dance competitions offered a vivid portrayal of the islands' character. The celebration was not merely a show; it was a reflection of the pride and passion that differentiate the Tahitian people.

6. Homestays and Community Engagement:
Personal Experience:

Staying at a local homestay allowed me to experience daily life in French Polynesia. From acquiring traditional culinary techniques to joining in community events, I felt that the warmth of the people was as much a part of the experience as the stunning scenery.

7. Language and Storytelling:
Personal Experience:
Learning a few Tahitian words enabled me to connect on a deeper level with the people. over talks and tales, I received insights into the oral traditions that have been passed down over ages, preserving the islands' history and wisdom.

Cultural immersion in the archipelago is an opportunity to transcend beyond the position of a tourist and become a participant in the living narrative of French Polynesia.
It's a recognition that the landscapes are not only scenery, but a canvas upon which the

culture is built. As you partake in ancient ceremonies, share jokes, and listen to the music of the islands, you'll find that the essence of French Polynesia resides not only in its natural beauty but in the spirit of its people and the history of its customs.

# Chapter 8. Practical Tips

## Language and Communication

**Language and Communication in French Polynesia: A Tapestry of Tongues**

In the midst of the South Pacific, French Polynesia weaves a stunning tapestry of languages that depict the islands' rich history, cultural fusion, and the joyful coexistence of cultures. Language here is more than a tool for communication; it's a key that unlocks the doors to grasping the numerous levels of Tahitian identity. Join me as we dive extensively into the domain of language and communication in French Polynesia, analysing its nuances and relevance.

1. Tahitian: The Heartbeat of Culture:

Nuance and Inflection:

Tahitian, the indigenous language, is the pulse of culture. Its smooth cadence and melodic inflection depict the islands' rhythms and the people's connectedness to their environment. From greetings to proverbs, every word is a brushstroke that builds a picture of the Tahitian way of life.

## 2. French: A Lingua Franca:

Cultural Fusion:

French, as a result of colonisation, is widely spoken and retains cultural relevance. It's not only a means of communication; it's a symbol of the islands' rich heritage. The coexistence of French and Tahitian displays the compatibility of civilizations and the persistence of the Tahitian people.

## 3. Multilingualism: A Reflection of Diversity:

Personal Experience:

Engaging in dialogues in French Polynesia, I marveled at the easy transitions between languages. Locals effortlessly shifted between Tahitian, French, and often English to accommodate the diverse backgrounds of visitors. This multilingualism spoke loudly about the islands' hospitality and adaptability.

4. Unwritten Languages: Body and Nature:
Personal Experience:
Beyond spoken languages, I found that French Polynesia communicates through numerous techniques. The pace of ancient dances, the patterns of tattoo art, and the symbols of tapa cloth all tell narratives that transcend words. Even the rustling leaves and crashing waters seem to contain secrets that link with the soul.

5. Preserving Oral Traditions: Passing Down Wisdom:
Cultural Heritage:
Language plays a key function in perpetuating the islands' oral traditions. Elders pass down myths, legends, and

historical records through storytelling. These stories not only entertain but also carry the wisdom of generations, preserving a sense of identity and belonging.

## 6. Language as a Bridge:
Personal Experience:
As I fumbled through my first Tahitian phrases, folks smiled pleasantly and embraced my attempts to connect. Even with limited vocabulary, I knew that language is a bridge that links people together. It's not about fluency; it's about the effort to understand and be understood.

## 7. A Living Heritage:
Cultural Evolution:
Language in French Polynesia is a living heritage that continues to evolve. Younger generations are seeking to maintain the languages alive by enrolling in language programs and cultural events. The islands' languages are not relegated to the past; they impact the present and future.

Language and communication in French Polynesia are more than words; they are threads that weave the islands' unique cultural fabric. Through each spoken syllable, dance step, and traditional motif, the people of French Polynesia express a story of resilience, togetherness, and a profound connection to the land and ocean. As you interact with the languages of the archipelago, you'll realise that understanding the languages is like recognising the essence of the islands themselves — a treasure mine of information, diversity, and shared humanity.

## Respectful Travel Etiquette and Local Customs

## Respectful Travel Etiquette and Local Customs: Navigating with Cultural Sensitivity

Exploring French Polynesia goes beyond its magnificent nature; it's a tour into a world with rich cultural heritage and local customs that deserve recognition and respect. Navigating these islands with cultural knowledge is not simply a courtesy; it's a means to appreciate the communities that call these paradises home. Join me as we dive deeper into the subject of polite travel etiquette and local customs in French Polynesia, learning how to walk lightly and make the most of your vacation.

1. Greeting with an Aloha Spirit:
Cultural Nuance:
Greeting locals with a pleasant "ia ora na" or "maeva" is a reflection of the islands' kindness. Taking the time to identify folks with a genuine smile and a courteous comment goes a long way in developing

connections and expressing respect for local customs.

2. Dressing Modestly:
Cultural Sensitivity:
When visiting communities and religious places, dressed modestly is a sign of respect. Wearing attire that covers shoulders and knees is acceptable, as it fits with the islands' cultural norms and displays an awareness of local values.

3. Removing Shoes:
Cultural Gesture:
In many homes, guesthouses, and even some public settings, removing shoes before entering is normal. This gesture appreciates the cleanliness of indoor locations and is a means to exhibit respect for the living spaces of the people.

4. Seeking Permission:
Cultural Courtesy:

Before taking photos of persons or their property, seeking permission is not only polite but also respectful of their privacy. Engaging in a brief chat before snapping a photo communicates that you respect their permission.

5. Preserving Nature and Marine Life:
Environmental Respect:
The ocean and land are vital to Tahitian culture. While snorkeling and exploring, avoid touching or disturbing aquatic animals and coral reefs. Participating in eco-friendly activities and acknowledging conservation projects helps to the islands' sustainability.

6. Supporting Local Economy:
Community Engagement:
Shopping at local markets, eating at family-owned cafés, and purchasing handicrafts directly from artisans contribute to the local economy. By interacting with the community, you're not merely a visitor;

you're an ally in the preservation of their way of life.

7. Participating in Local Traditions:
Cultural Involvement:
When invited, join in traditional rites, dances, and festivals. Whether it's weaving, cooking, or learning about navigation, partaking in encourages you to immerse yourself in the culture and expresses your enthusiasm for its practises.

8. Language & Communication:
Cultural Respect:
Using basic Tahitian phrases like "ia ora na" (hello) and "māuruuru" (thank you) communicates that you're making an effort to connect. Locals like when visitors take the effort to engage in their language and culture.

Respectful travel etiquette and regard to local customs in French Polynesia is not just about fitting in; it's about recognising the people, their traditions, and the nation that welcomes you. As you tour these islands with cultural knowledge, you'll notice that your experiences get deeper and more meaningful. By embracing the practises and beliefs of French Polynesia, you're not merely a tourist passing through; you're a guest who leaves behind lovely memories and a deep appreciation for the tapestry of cultures that call these islands home.

## Health and Safety Advice

### Health and Safety in French Polynesia: Nurturing Your Well-Being

Embarking on a vacation to French Polynesia is an opportunity to explore, learn, and create lifetime memories. To thoroughly savour this event, it's vital to highlight health and safety. From understanding local healthcare facilities to enjoying outdoor adventure appropriately, let's delve deeper into the arena of health and safety in French Polynesia, insuring your well-being while immersing yourself in paradise.

1. Pre-Travel Health Precautions:
Medical Consultation:
Before your departure, plan a consultation with your healthcare provider to discuss immunisations, medications, and any health concerns. Ensuring your health is perfect before flying is a proactive step towards a safe flight.

2. Travel Insurance:
Coverage and Protection:
Acquiring comprehensive travel insurance that includes medical coverage is vital. In the event of unanticipated illness, accident, or travel issues, having insurance offers piece of mind and assures you obtain the care you need.

3. Sun Protection:
Skin Health:

The sun's intensity in French Polynesia may be strong. Apply and reapply sunscreen with a high SPF, wear protective garments, and don a wide-brimmed hat to preserve your skin from hazardous UV rays.

4. Hydration and Safe Consumption:
Water and Beverages:
Staying hydrated is crucial in the tropical climate. Opt for bottled or filtered water, and be cautious when drinking ice or tap water. Enjoying local coconut water or fresh fruit juices is an excellent way to be hydrated.

5. Insect Precautions:
Protection against Mosquitoes:
Mosquitoes may be common in various places. Use insect repellent, wear long sleeves and pants at dawn and dusk, and consider sleeping beneath a mosquito net to decrease the risk of mosquito-borne infections.

6. Responsible Outdoor Exploration:
Adventure Safety:
While experiencing the islands' natural beauties, engage in outdoor activities wisely. Whether it's hiking, snorkeling, or diving, keep to safety regulations, obey local limits, and seek the services of certified guides for more rigorous experiences.

7. Respect for Marine Life:
Coral and Wildlife Conservation:
When snorkeling or diving, avoid touching or standing on coral reefs. Interacting with marine species should be done with respect and care to assure both your safety and the preservation of the vulnerable ecosystems.

8. Staying Informed:
Local Knowledge:
Stay updated on meteorological conditions, especially during hurricane season. In the event of any weather-related warnings or alerts, follow local authorities' instructions to ensure your safety.

9. Emergency Contacts and Healthcare:
Local Resources:
Familiarize oneself with the location of neighbouring medical institutes, hospitals, and clinics. Keep emergency contact information immediately accessible, and know how to get medical help if necessary.

Prioritizing health and safety in French Polynesia improves your holiday, allowing you to thoroughly immerse yourself in the islands' beauty while minimising dangers. By taking proactive measures, being informed, and being sensitive to your well-being, you'll establish a foundation that enables you to make the most of your trip, relishing each minute in paradise with a sense of security and confidence.

# Chapter 9. Memories and Souvenirs

## Capturing Your Tahitian Journey

**Capturing Your Tahitian Journey: Preserving Memories in Paradise**

French Polynesia's beauty is a canvas waiting to be painted with the strokes of your experiences. Capturing your Tahitian trip by photography, writing, and other creative ways helps you to retain the moments that connect with your heart. Let's dive completely into the art of preserving your Tahitian adventure, ensuring that the memories you make become permanent treasures.

1. Photography as a Visual Diary:
Personal Experience:

Every daybreak above the turquoise lagoon, every magnificent tapa design, and every pleasant individual you encounter is a snapshot of your adventure. Use your camera to construct a narrative - from the busy marketplaces to the tranquil beaches, each shot becomes a page in the visual book of your adventure.

2. The Magic of Sunrise and Sunset:
Natural Spectacles:
Tahiti's sunrises and sunsets are like living paintings, generating gorgeous colours that beautify the sky. Wake up early to enjoy the first rays of dawn over the water, and then select a great position to see the sun melting into the horizon at sunset.

3. Cultural Encounters & Traditions:
Visual Storytelling:
Capture the essence of Tahitian culture by documenting traditional dance performances, local artisans at work, and sacred marae places. These images not only

make a visual narrative but also help you to share the depth of the culture with others.

4. Underwater Wonders:
Personal Experience:
Equip yourself with a waterproof camera to record the stunning underwater world. Snorkeling and diving images portray the vibrant coral reefs, curious aquatic life, and the sense of weightlessness that marks the experience.

5. Portraits of People and Smiles:
Human Connections:
People are an important component of your journey. Photographing the warm smiles of locals, the laughter shared with other visitors, and the friendships created along the journey immortalizes the bonds you've made.

6. A Fusion of Flavors:
Food Photography:

Tahitian cuisine is a piece of art. Capture the colours and textures of exotic fruits, the ornate presentation of traditional dinners, and the gourmet delights that thrill your taste buds.

7. Incorporating Local Elements:
Creative Composition:
Use local materials such as seashells, tapa cloth, and vibrant flowers to boost the arrangement of your photographs. These qualities provide depth and authenticity to your visual narrative.

8. Keeping a Travel Journal:
Personal Reflections:
In addition to photography, keeping a travel journal enables you to share your ideas, emotions, and observations in words. Describe the aromas, sounds, and sensations that accompany your experiences, forming a literary vision of your travel.

9. Balancing Technology and Presence: Immersive Experiences:
While preserving experiences is vital, attempt to establish a balance between documenting and being entirely present. Put down the camera occasionally to immerse yourself in the sights, sounds, and sensations of Tahiti.

Capturing your Tahitian journey is an art that goes beyond just taking photographs. It's about presenting the essence of the islands - the beauty, the culture, and the connections – in visual and textual form. Whether through photography, journaling, or a combination of both, your creative creations will become cherished memories that bring back the beauty of your experience every time you return them.

## Meaningful Souvenirs & Keepsakes

**Meaningful Souvenirs & Keepsakes from Tahiti: Treasures of the Heart**

Bringing a piece of Tahiti back with you is not just about acquiring stuff; it's about capturing the essence of your visit and the sensations it inspired. Meaningful memories and keepsakes are like time capsules that carry you back to the beauty, culture, and people you experienced. Let's go extensively into the area of choosing and cherishing souvenirs from Tahiti, ensuring that the gems you bring home are actually jewels of the heart.

1. Handcrafted Artistry:
Tapa Cloth and Carvings:
Tapa cloth, decorated with gorgeous designs, and hand-carved wooden artefacts symbolise Tahitian craftsmanship. These relics symbolise the islands' culture and may be shown as exquisite art or useful décor.

2. Black Pearls:
Natural Elegance:

Tahiti is famed for its stunning black pearls. Each pearl is a unique product of nature, representing elegance and beauty. As jewelry or displayed in a unique container, black pearls convey the magic of the ocean's depths.

### 3. Fragrance of Monoi Oil:
Sensual Reminders:
Monoi oil, mixed with the perfume of Tahitian gardenia, transmits the essence of the islands. Use it as a perfumed remembrance of your vacation or to enrich your regular routine with a touch of Tahitian beauty.

### 4. Local Art:
Visual Memories:
Paintings, sculptures, and other sorts of local art allow you to take a part of Tahiti's beauty home with you. Choose works that correspond with your experiences, serving as visual memories that transcend time.

### 5. Traditional Instruments:
Melodies of Tahiti:
Bring the sounds of Tahiti into your home by acquiring traditional instruments like ukuleles or drums. Display them as lovely artefacts or learn to play, letting the music to carry you back to the islands.

### 6. Culinary Delights:
Flavors of the Islands:
Spices, vanilla beans, and local preserves may be wonderful souvenirs for culinary lovers. Infuse your cuisine with the flavours of Tahiti and relive your culinary trips through your creations.

### 7. Personal Creations:
Artistic Endeavors:
Create your own mementos by taking workshops where you may manufacture your tapa cloth, weave baskets, or learn traditional dance. The goods you develop will have not simply aesthetic merit but also personal memories.

8. Meaningful Jewelry:
Symbolism & Sentiment:
Select jewelry that holds special importance, whether it's a Tahitian motif, a shell pendant, or an item that remembers you of a certain moment or connection during your trip.

9. Captured Moments:
Personalized Souvenirs:
Turn your own photographs into tangible mementos like photo albums, posters, or personalised calendars. These items allow you to relive your journey through your own view.

Meaningful souvenirs and keepsakes from Tahiti are more than products; they're containers that carry memories, emotions, and connections. When choosing these treasures, consider the thoughts they stir, the experiences they reflect, and the narratives they carry. By bringing home these impassioned presents, you're not only collecting souvenirs; you're constructing a physical link to the delight of your holiday, guaranteeing that the beauty and spirit of Tahiti remain alive in your heart and surroundings.

# Chapter 10. Conclusion

## Reflecting on Your Tahiti Adventure

### Reflecting on Your Tahiti Adventure: Unveiling the Essence of the Journey

As your Tahiti adventure draws to an end, the time comes to reflect on the moments that have filled your soul and the experiences that have weaved eternal memories. Reflection is a means to extract the essence of your trip, to savour the beauty and wisdom it has offered, and to carry its lessons forward. Let's dig completely into the art of reflecting on your Tahiti holiday, allowing you to discover the deeper layers of your experiences.

1. Finding Quiet Moments:
Contemplation and Stillness:

Find a tranquil spot — maybe a quiet beach, a hillside, or a comfy corner – where you may be alone with your thoughts. In the tranquil embrace of nature, allow your thoughts to emerge spontaneously.

2. Gratitude for Connections:
Human Encounters:
Reflect on the persons you've encountered - locals, other travelers, and those who shared their story with you. Consider the speeches that enlarged your outlook and the relationships that touched your heart.

3. Moments of Awe:
Nature's Beauty:
Recall the moments that snatched your breath away - the blazing sunsets, the blue lagoons, and the lush landscapes. Reflect on how these sights touched your spirit and left an imprint on your soul.

4. Lessons from Challenges:
Personal Growth:

Consider the challenges you faced throughout your travel. Reflect on how you navigated them and the lessons you acquired. Challenges usually contain hidden gems of growth and endurance.

5. Cultural Insights:
Understanding and Empathy:
Think about the cultural immersion you had - the traditions, the cuisine, and the interactions with the local inhabitants. Reflect on the insights received and how they boosted your understanding of the world.

6. Moments of Presence:
Mindful Experiences:
Recall the times you were entirely there - when you watched the waves lap the shore, appreciated a meal, or engaged in a debate without interruption. Reflect on how these events strengthened your connection to the present.

## 7. Revisiting Journals and Photos:
Visual and Written Memories:
Review your travel record and the photographs you gathered. Allow the written words and imagery to transport you back to the sensations and ideas you experienced in those moments.

## 8. Insights about Yourself:
Self-Discovery:
Reflect on how your travel has altered your outlook, values, and sense of self. Consider the components of your character that were emphasised during your vacation in Tahiti.

## 9. Cultivating Gratitude:
Appreciating the Experience:
Cultivate appreciation for the complete route – the highs and lows, the fortunate moments, and the intentional choices. Reflect on how this journey has impacted your life.

## 10. Carrying the Essence Forward:

Integrating the Experience:
Consider how you may transmit the spirit of your Tahiti trip into your daily life. Reflect on the ways you may combine the lessons acquired, the connections made, and the beauty encountered into your continued journey.

Reflecting on your Tahiti vacation is a chance to recognise the experiences that have formed you. It's a chance to distill the journey's essence, extracting ideas and experiences that will remain with you long after you've returned home. As you think, you'll find that your time in Tahiti wasn't merely a succession of events; it was a transformational trip that continues to grow within you, leading your route with new clarity and appreciation.

## Embracing the Spirit of French Polynesia

## Embracing the Spirit of French Polynesia: Nurturing the Soul of Paradise

French Polynesia isn't simply a place; it's a state of mind, a way of being, and a spirit that resonates within anyone who experience its beauty. Embracing the spirit of French Polynesia is about more than visiting; it's about immersing yourself in the essence of the islands and allowing its beauty, culture, and calm to touch your soul. Let's go deeper into the art of embracing the spirit of French Polynesia, urging you to become a part of the islands' timeless fabric.

1. Embracing Nature's Rhythms:
Connected to the Elements:
French Polynesia's soul is linked with the natural environment. Rise with the sun, listen to the quiet lapping of waves, and feel the breeze rustling through the palm trees. By synchronising with nature's cycles, you become attuned to the pulse of the islands.

2. Slowing Down and Savoring:
Cultivating Tranquility:
In the islands, time appears to slow down. Embrace this pace by relishing each moment - from leisurely strolls on the beach to slow chats over meals. By accepting the slow flow, you welcome peace into your days.

3. Cultivating Respect:
Honoring the Land and Culture:
Show respect for the land, the people, and the culture. Engage in cultural activities, learn about local traditions, and treat the islands with care. By expressing regard, you become a keeper of the islands' spirit.

4. Gratitude for Simplicity:
Finding Joy in Basics:
French Polynesia encourages us to discover happiness in simple pleasures. A fresh coconut, a brilliant sunset, or a friendly welcome from a native may provide

enormous delight. By practising thankfulness for the necessities, you enter into the islands' attitude of serenity.

## 5. Embracing Community:
Connections with Locals:
Interact with locals, discover their tales, and partake in their customs. By being a member of the community, you tap into the islands' spirit of welcome and togetherness.

## 6. Mindful Exploration:
Presence in Every Step:
Whether swimming in bright seas or wandering through local marketplaces, be totally present in each encounter. By practising mindfulness, you build a profound connection with the present and the spirit of the islands.

## 7. Reconnecting with Your Essence:
Inner Reflection:
Use the islands' tranquillity as a background for reflection. Embrace seclusion on a

peaceful beach or in a tranquil garden, letting your inner thoughts and emotions to surface and harmonise with the spirit of the environment.

8. Infusing Beauty into Everyday:
Art of Aesthetics:
Bring the islands' aesthetic into your life — adorn your room with tropical themes, wear vibrant materials, or prepare Tahitian-inspired foods. By pouring beauty into your surroundings, you represent the islands' spirit of craftsmanship.

9. Carrying the Spirit Forward:
Legacy of the Islands:
As you leave French Polynesia, carry its spirit within you. Let the islands' lessons in simplicity, mindfulness, and connection lead your journey beyond the archipelago.

Embracing the essence of French Polynesia isn't just about a holiday; it's about a change. It's about letting the islands' energy to enter your being, influencing the way you perceive the world, and nourishing your soul with their ageless beauty and wisdom. By immersing yourself in this atmosphere, you become a part of the islands' history — a custodian of their charm, a traveler changed, and a soul permanently tied to the heart of paradise.

Maps

1. Google Maps: A dependable and comprehensive map service that gives directions, areas of interest, and street views.
Website: [Google Maps](https://www.google.com/maps)

2. Maps.Me: A user-friendly offline map tool that enables you to download maps for your location and utilise them without an internet connection.
Website: [Maps.Me](https://maps.me)

3. OpenStreetMap: An open-source map service that gives precise and up-to-date maps generated by volunteers worldwide. Website: [OpenStreetMap](https://www.openstreet map.org)

4. Tahiti and French Polynesia Maps: Some travel guidebooks or websites specialized to Tahiti and French Polynesia may give comprehensive maps particular to the islands and attractions.

5. Local Tourist Offices: Many tourist offices in Tahiti and the neighboring islands offer tangible maps and brochures with local information and areas of interest.

Made in United States
Troutdale, OR
03/04/2024

18206922R00071